Harry Potter™

ARAGOG

A BEHIND-THE-SCENES LOOK
AT THE ACROMANTULA ON FILM

INCREDI
BUILDS

A Division of Insight Editions, LP
San Rafael, California

INTRODUCTION

Aragog is an Acromantula and the patriarch of a cluster of these menacing spiders who live in the Forbidden Forest. Aragog was brought to Hogwarts by Rubeus Hagrid when he was a student, many years before the events of *Harry Potter and the Chamber of Secrets*. His beloved pet was unfairly accused by another student, Tom Marvolo Riddle, of being the monster that killed a student when the Chamber of Secrets was first opened, but Aragog was able to escape into the forest. Harry Potter and Ron Weasley seek out Aragog and his descendants— who literally descend on them—when Hagrid suggests Aragog can help them with information about the Heir.

Sadly, Aragog passes away from old age during the events of *Harry Potter and the Half-Blood Prince*. Potions professor Horace Slughorn delivers a touching eulogy for him, but not before he asks permission to extract some highly rare (and valuable) Acromantula venom.

"I came to Hagrid from a distant land, in the pocket of a traveller."

—ARAGOG, HARRY POTTER AND THE CHAMBER OF SECRETS

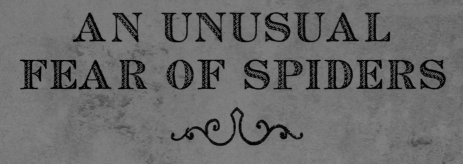

AN UNUSUAL
FEAR OF SPIDERS

There have been big spiders in movies before, and as author J.K. Rowling admits, "You see these old sci-fi movies where they have spiders, and they're always hysterically funny; they're never, never scary." What worried the author in this case was how the filmmakers would create a huge spider that would be as frightening as she had imagined and not laughable. *Harry Potter and the Chamber of Secrets* director Chris Columbus felt the same way: "Aragog worked wonderfully in the book, but it was the one creature we were terrified about designing because a talking spider gets into a cheesy territory." So the filmmakers knew that while they could have fun creating the creature, they had to make sure no one was laughing when Aragog was on-screen!

"*If anybody was looking for some stuff, then all they'd have to do would be to follow the spiders. That'd lead 'em right! That's all I'm sayin'.*"

—RUBEUS HAGRID, *HARRY POTTER AND THE CHAMBER OF SECRETS*

HIDING IN THE HOLLOWS

One way director Chris Columbus knew he could keep Aragog from being comical was to keep him in the shadows. "I knew that if we were in a brightly lit situation the audience would be laughing at this talking spider," Chris says. So Aragog's lair was set deep inside the dark Forbidden Forest. Spider's Hollow was placed under a domed canopy of highly exaggerated trees and branches, and draped in layers and layers of cobwebs.

"Why spiders? Why couldn't it be follow the butterflies?"

—RON WEASLEY,
HARRY POTTER AND THE CHAMBER OF SECRETS

TWO DIMENSIONS

Every creature design begins with two-dimensional visual development sketches and paintings created by the art department. For Aragog, real spiders were researched and it was the look of a wolf spider that inspired *Harry Potter and the Chamber of Secrets* conceptual artist Adam Brockbank. "When you scale up a wolf spider to Aragog's size," Adam admits, "they're pretty scary-looking creatures!"

WEB DESIGN

Concept art of the creature placed into its environment can suggest possible lighting and staging as the set is being constructed. In the case of Spider's Hollow, artists Adam Brockbank, Dermot Power and Andrew Williamson created haunting and very webby landscapes for Aragog, and also imagined his first meeting with Harry and Ron. The visual artists also made use of computers in their work and could offer different combinations of landscapes, characters and creatures for the filmmakers to consider.

THREE DIMENSIONS

Once the concept art was approved, it was up to creature effects supervisor Nick Dudman and his team to make a three-dimensional version of Aragog. "Each creature is sculpted into a series of small tabletop models—called maquettes—for review," Nick explains. With these, the director, producers and especially production designer Stuart Craig, who oversaw everything in the Harry Potter films, get a chance to see the creature from "all sides" and offer tweaks before a much larger maquette is made if needed.

Digital Dimensions

Once its design is approved, the filmmakers have to consider if a creature should be constructed in a computer (CG, or computer-generated) or in a life-size animatronic form. "Aragog was something that I really fought to be done physically," says creature effects supervisor Nick Dudman. "When the idea of CG came up, I said no, no, no! We knew there'd be spiders everywhere, running all over the place and sliding down webs. But when I read the script, I thought, well, all Aragog does is climb out of a hole, deliver some dialogue and that's that. We can build that. All those other spiders running up and down in the trees, yes, absolutely, digital. But we could and should build Aragog."

NOT AN ITSY-BITSY SPIDER

The Aragog seen in *Harry Potter and the Chamber of Secrets* had an eighteen-foot leg span and weighed a ton. It took a team of twenty-five people a total of five months to build the elephant-sized Acromantula. Nick Dudman remembers standing on the set when Aragog shot his scenes: "I saw a giant spider walk out of a hole and deliver dialogue, for real, in front of me! Not a camera trick!" Nick admits that one of the reasons he does what he does is because "frankly, it's just great fun!"

CREATURE COMMITTEE

Creature effects supervisor Nick Dudman knows that the first version of any creature is never its last. "I always listen to everything my crew has to say about the creatures we create," Nick explains. But he also listens to more than just the crew: "Anyone's opinion is valid. If the caterers see it and say, 'Don't you think the legs should be longer?' we'll consider it. If a bunch of kids visit and say, 'That's horrible!' we know we're okay. But if somebody sees it and laughs, I want to know why. It's not a machine you're worried about; it's a *character* you're worried about. By the time the creature reaches the set, it's been 'designed' by a huge number of people. So if it looks real and behaves real, that's why."

MAKING IT WORK

A creature's function is just as important to its design as its look. "You can have all the best ideas in the world, from everybody,"

says Nick Dudman, "but it's only when you stick two bits of something together that you realise, hmm, I think we need an extra joint in there. Hmm, I need this to extend much more this way than that way." Nick consults with the lighting and set designers to determine a creature's look. He says, "The set could be very dark. So maybe what we should do is fur him two shades lighter than we think he should be, knowing we can airbrush darker where we want, but at least he'll show up." Aragog evolved and changed right down to the moment he was placed on the set.

ARANIA EXUMAI!

"Go? I think not. My sons and daughters do not harm Hagrid, on my command. But I cannot deny them fresh meat when it wanders so willingly into our midst. Good-bye, friend of Hagrid."

—ARAGOG, *HARRY POTTER AND THE CHAMBER OF SECRETS*

Harry Potter and Ron Weasley are surrounded by the numerous offspring of Aragog in *Harry Potter and the Chamber of Secrets*, who consider the students a tasty meal. How do they escape? Harry uses the *Arania Exumai* spell which blasts the spiders back and away. Harry saw the spell in action when Tom Riddle's diary showed him a memory of Tom's confrontation with Hagrid, when he accused Hagrid's pet spider of being the Heir of Slytherin. The spell was among eight new spells created for this film.

A RUFF ESCAPE

Harry and Ron are rescued from the Acromantula attack by the Weasleys' Flying Ford Anglia, which has been living rough in the Forbidden Forest since it fled the Whomping Willow. Hagrid's dog, Fang, who accompanied them into the forest, leaps in before the car drives away. "You couldn't put a real dog in the back," says creature effects supervisor Nick Dudman. "So we created a 'stunt' dog that was radio-controlled to move." The creature was also programmed to drool, which Dudman explains with a wink, they "put in just to upset Rupert."

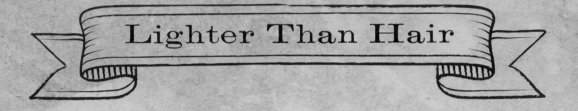
The life-size Aragog model was created using Latex and polyfoam materials that are easy to manoeuvre. The maquette was airbrushed to colour its legs, head and body, and then it was "flocked." This involves a team of people who "shoot" small fuzzy hairs onto a creature in a very complicated process. But a large spider also has very large hairs. Another team inserted the larger spider hairs one by one all over Aragog, employing a special needle. Broom hairs were used for the finer ones. The bigger, even hairier hairs were made using the centre of a feather that had been dabbed with adhesive fluff and dragged through Lurex, a type of yarn with a metallic finish.

ALL WET

Many of the large animatronic creatures you see in films are operated via a hydraulic system, which uses oil pumped through cables to create movement. "Hydraulic movement is very jerky," creature effects supervisor Nick Dudman explains. "But spiders are slow and graceful." So Nick replaced the oil with water. "In tests, it looked exactly like that horrible, quiet way spiders move just before they run." The creature department built all of Aragog's animatronic parts using what Nick dubbed *aquatronics*. "It leaked occasionally," he admits, "but it was definitely creepy."

NO STRINGS ATTACHED

Aragog's mechanical forelegs were operated using a motion-control device called a "waldo." A waldo is a small, handheld replica of an object or creature that is connected wirelessly to the full-size version. The waldo's controller moves the miniature, which then causes the creature to reproduce the actions. "At the back of the set," explains creature effects supervisor Nick Dudman, "we had a small set of spider legs. And whatever we did with those four legs physically, the legs on the real spider would do." Think of it like a puppeteer who can make a marionette move without using any strings!

SPIDER ON A STICK

Aragog's rear four legs were operated by puppeteers. In order for Aragog to climb out of his hollow, Nick Dudman's team placed the spider on a counterweight system. "We had Aragog on one end of what is basically a seesaw," Nick explains, "and there was a counterweight on the other end." Four performers manipulated Aragog's legs with, as Nick describes it, "basically a stick hanging out of the bottom." Aragog was placed into a deep depression on the sound stage, and when Aragog was tipped up by the puppeteers, he literally walked forward.

SPEAK UP!

Being able to physically interact with life-size moving creatures during filming is a real advantage for the actors. Aragog's creators went a step further and installed a voice-activated system in Aragog's mouth which was linked to a computer. When the computer played a sound file of Aragog's dialogue, voiced by actor Julian Glover, Aragog's mouth would "lip-synch" the words! All the operators needed to do was press pause after Aragog's lines and the young actors would speak theirs. This meant that Daniel Radcliffe (Harry Potter) and Rupert Grint (Ron Weasley) could act in real time with the Acromantula.

A BAD FIRST IMPRESSION

*"Seriously misunderstood creatures, spiders are.
It's the eyes, I reckon. They unnerve some folk."*

—RUBEUS HAGRID,
HARRY POTTER AND THE HALF-BLOOD PRINCE

Daniel Radcliffe (Harry Potter) remembers his first meeting with Aragog: "We did our first shot in Spider's Hollow, where me and Rupert walked over to this ledge in the forest. We got over there, and there's a jillion-ton mechanical spider waiting for us on the other side. And it had these amazing pincers that kept moving. It was very creepy!"

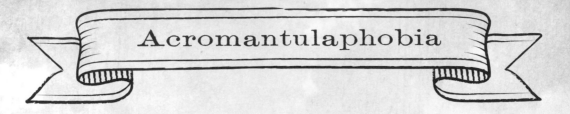

Acromantulaphobia

Rupert Grint (Ron Weasley) remembers his first meeting with Aragog a little differently. "It was horrible!" he says. Rupert has a fear of spiders similar to his character's: "I didn't know what to expect. I don't like spiders in real life. I even get really scared of rubber ones. We come into the hollow, and we see this spider that's the size of an elephant. It really did make me feel uneasy. When I saw Aragog for the first time, I wasn't acting; I was genuinely scared." Rupert admits that it's his least favourite scene in the movie, and he still can't watch it all the way through. "Filming that didn't help my fear at all!"

SAME REACTION

Creature effects supervisor Nick Dudman also recalls shooting with Aragog and the two young actors. "Daniel kept saying, 'I don't want to be near that.' And Rupert absolutely freaked." Nick was sympathetic to the boys' reactions but was, at the same time, satisfied, because "they were not reacting to the fear of being next to a large mechanical thing. When cast or crew members didn't like it, it was because it was a spider. It gave them the same feeling a real spider would give."

> "*I . . . don't . . . like . . . spiders.*"
>
> —RON WEASLEY,
> *HARRY POTTER AND THE CHAMBER OF SECRETS*

FAREWELL, ARAGOG

Several years later, during the events of *Harry Potter and the Half-Blood Prince*, Harry Potter drinks a small vial of the liquid luck potion—*Felix Felicis*—that he won in Potions class and meets up with Professor Horace Slughorn. Together, they come upon Hagrid presiding at the funeral of Aragog, who has died of old age. Here, the professor gets the unexpected opportunity to acquire some Acromantula venom before the spider's burial. It is after this sad assembly that Harry's luck changes in his task of collecting Slughorn's true memory of how Tom Riddle learned about creating Horcruxes.

"*Hagrid. The last thing I wish to be is indelicate, but Acromantula venom is uncommonly rare. Would you allow me to extract a vial or two—purely for academic purposes, you understand . . .*"

—PROFESSOR HORACE SLUGHORN,
HARRY POTTER AND THE HALF-BLOOD PRINCE

SO, WHAT DOES IT DO?

As with *Harry Potter and the Chamber of Secrets*, the subject of whether Aragog would be a physical model or a computer-generated character came up for *Harry Potter and the Half-Blood Prince*. So questions were asked: Which is more economical? Will it be easy to use on the set? Will it give something to the actors that would make all the difference if it wasn't there? "I always fight to do it practically if it makes sense," says creature effects supervisor Nick Dudman. "Of course, sometimes you can't do it animatronically; you have to do it digitally. I accept that. But when they told me that Aragog in *Half-Blood Prince* was dead, and it wasn't going to do anything, I thought, 'Let us just build him, please.'" So Aragog was another practical effect, with a few important upgrades.

A NEW OLD ARAGOG

"Had a family, I trust?"
"Oh, yeah."

—HORACE SLUGHORN AND HARRY POTTER,
HARRY POTTER AND THE HALF-BLOOD PRINCE

Nick Dudman looked forward to bringing Aragog back but knew that the original couldn't be used because this one would be lifeless and upside down. Aragog was redesigned to show the effects of his death. "I wanted for it to be translucent, like a dead, curled-up spider you would see in the bath," Nick explains. "When they catch the light, they look like they've gone hollow." This time, the husk of the creature was cast in a polyurethane material. "You can see the understructure of the creature through the surface when the evening light shines through his legs," Nick adds.

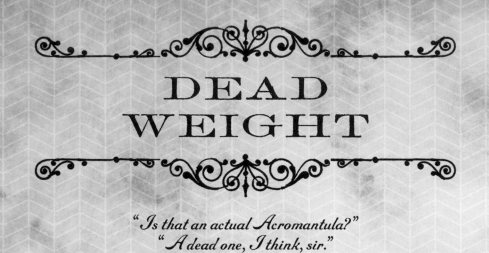

DEAD
WEIGHT

"Is that an actual Acromantula?"
"A dead one, I think, sir."

—PROFESSOR HORACE SLUGHORN AND HARRY POTTER, *HARRY POTTER AND THE HALF-BLOOD PRINCE*

The initial script for *Harry Potter and the Half-Blood Prince* called for Hagrid to push Aragog into a sloping hillside grave. "So, based on that, we had to make a strong, heavy version, because he had to move in the same way something heavy would move," says creature effects supervisor Nick Dudman. "If he'd been lighter, his legs would have floated about and it wouldn't have looked right." This time, the spider was built with a steel skeleton inside and was completely solid so that it wouldn't collapse when it was dropped. The three-quarter-ton creature was fastened to a track with a safety cable. "We filmed it landing in the pit, and it moved beautifully," Nick says. "I knew it'd be heavy, but I must admit it was heavier than I was expecting!"

A TOUCHING TRIBUTE

"Farewell, Aragog, king of the arachnids. The body will decay, but your spirit lingers on in your human friends . . ."

—EXCERPT FROM ARAGOG'S EULOGY BY HORACE SLUGHORN, *HARRY POTTER AND THE HALF-BLOOD PRINCE*

Aragog was such a beloved character to the film crew that they wore black armbands in sympathy while the spider's final scene was filmed. The crew also hadn't expected how much Aragog's eulogy would touch them. "Even an inanimate object can cause a truly emotive moment, which is nice," says Nick Dudman. "You know you've got it right when people react to the creature as if it's real."

MAKE IT YOUR OWN

One of the great things about IncrediBuilds models is that each one is completely customisable. The untreated natural wood can be decorated with paints, pencils, pens, beads, sequins—the list goes on and on!

Before you start building and decorating your model, read through the included instruction sheet so you understand how all the pieces come together. Then, choose a theme and make a plan. Do you want to make an exact replica of Aragog or something completely different? The choice is yours! Here is an example to get those creative juices flowing.

WHAT YOU'LL NEED

* Brown, orange, black, white, and cream acrylic paint
* Paintbrush
* Toothpick or fine-detail brush

TIPS BEFORE YOU BEGIN

* As a general rule of thumb, you'll want to use pens and pencils *before* building the model and paints *after* building the model.

* When making a replica, it's always good to study an actual image of what you are trying to copy. Look closely at the details throughout this book and brainstorm how you can re-create them.

PAINTING ARAGOG

① Assemble the model but leave the legs off.

② Paint the model and all of the legs brown.

③ Paint Aragog's front pincers with cream paint.

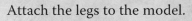

TIP: If you don't have cream paint, mix white paint with just a drop of brown paint.

④ Paint Aragog's eyes black. Remember, he has eight!

⑤ Use a toothpick or fine-detail brush to add white dots on top of the eyes you just painted.

⑥ Attach the legs to the model.

⑦ Now it's time to add Aragog's "fur." Using a toothpick or a fine-detail brush, add short, thin orange lines all over the model as shown. Start with one section and continue until Aragog is covered. Keep most of the lines going in the same direction. Around his face, though, the fur is matted, so go ahead and paint the lines in more than one direction.

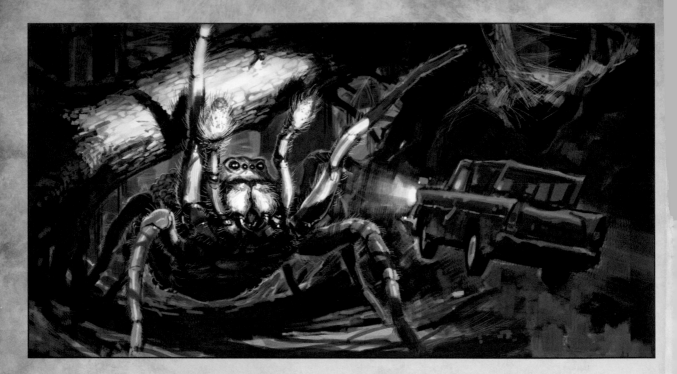

Copyright © 2020 Warner Bros. Entertainment Inc.
WIZARDING WORLD characters, names and related
indicia are © & ™ Warner Bros. Entertainment Inc.
WB SHIELD: © & ™ WBEI. Publishing Rights © JKR. (s20)

IncrediBuilds™
A Division of Insight Editions LP
PO Box 3088
San Rafael, CA 94912
www.insighteditions.com

Find us on Facebook: www.facebook.com/InsightEditions
Follow us on Twitter: @insighteditions

Published originally by Insight Editions, San Rafael, California, in 2016.
No part of this book may be reproduced in any form without written
permission from the publisher.

ISBN: 978-1-68298-022-4

Publisher: Raoul Goff
Art Director: Chrissy Kwasnik
Designer: Leah Bloise
Executive Editor: Vanessa Lopez
Project Editor: Greg Solano
Production Editor: Elaine Ou
Production Manager: Thomas Chung
Production Coordinator: Sam Taylor
Model Designer: Ryan Zhang

INSIGHT EDITIONS would like to thank Victoria Selover,
Melanie Swartz, Elaine Piechowski, Ashley Bol, Margo Guffin,
George Valdiviez and Kevin Morris.

Manufactured in China

iSeek Ltd, 1A Stairbridge Court, Bolney Grange Business Park,
Haywards Heath, RH17 5PA, UK.
12 Lower Hatch Street, Dublin, D02 R68, Ireland.